Ancient Egypt

A Guide to the Gods, Pharaohs, Dynasties and Traditions of Ancient Egypt

Table of Contents

Introduction 1
Chapter 1: Daily Life in Ancient Egypt 7
Chapter 2: Pyramids and Monuments of Egypt 16
Chapter 3: Religion, Gods, and Beliefs 24
Chapter 4: Burial Customs 32
Chapter 5: Animals, Beliefs, and Mummification 38
Chapter 6: Festivals 44
Chapter 7: Pharaohs and Dynasties 48
Chapter 8: Separating Truth from Fiction 57
Conclusion 61

Introduction

What makes Egypt so fascinating to us that there is a branch of archaeology called Egyptology? What did the ancient Egyptian culture have that makes it worth studying? Sun, sand, and pyramids await visitors in Egypt today, but what about the civilizations Egypt was built on? What did they find 5000 years ago to make them want to build a life in Egypt? To understand Ancient Egypt, one must also have a basis in time. When did the first settlers arrive in Egypt? When were the first pyramids erected? When did the first Pharaoh start ruling Egypt as a country in its own right? All of these questions and more will be answered for you, to help you understand that sometimes history has lessons for us- perhaps forgotten lessons that need to be brought back.

A Timeline of Ancient Egypt

Ancient Egypt is considered to be the period in time from 5000 BC to 332 BC. Little is known about the pre-dynastic period because few records exist. However, the period lasted for nearly 2000 years. Civilizations cropped up around the Nile and in Northern Africa along other water sources. These communities were based on agriculture and hunting. Trade between the groups occurred in order to share resources, and it opened the way for arts and crafts, politics, religion, and technology to develop.

Approximately 300 years before the pre-dynastic period ended in 3100, two kingdoms rose to power. One was called the Red Land, which was in the north of Egypt along the Nile River Delta, perhaps extending as far as what is now Atfih. The other kingdom was the White Land in the south, which was probably the area between Atfih and Gebel es-Silsila.

Did you know: Hollywood movies like The Mummy and The Mummy Returns are based on facts pulled from Ancient Egyptian history. The King of the southern kingdom was known as Scorpion. Scorpion tried to conquer the Red Land in 3200BC. However, he was not successful.

It was a century later before the two kingdoms would become one under King Menes. King Menes assumed the title of Pharaoh, which meant King in Egyptian, and he ruled over the first dynasty of Egypt.

King Menes began the Archaic Period, which lasted from 3100 to 2686 BC. King Menes lived and ruled Egypt in White Walls. White Walls, now called Memphis, was the capital of Ancient Egypt. It rests on the apex of the Nile River's delta. It was this capital that arose as a metropolis, dominating Egyptian society during the Old Kingdom Period. It was this period that was responsible for founding the Egyptian Society, the ideology of kingship and the religious beliefs in the gods like Horus. Irrigation, fertilization and better farming were discovered during this period.

Egypt is broken into periods by archaeologists. The next periods were as follows:

- Old Kingdom - 2686 to 2181 BC
- First Intermediate Period - 2181 to 2055 BC
- Middle Kingdom – The 12th Dynasty - 2055 to 1786 BC
- Second Intermediate Period - 1786 to 1567 BC
- New Kingdom - 1567 to 1085 BC
- Third Intermediate Period - 1085 to 664 BC

- Late Period - 664 to 332 BC

Most of the following chapters will concentrate on the Old Kingdom period. It is the age of the pyramid builders, and it is also considered the third dynasty of Pharaohs. You might recognize a few names from this period such as Imhotep, who was highlighted in the Hollywood films. King Djoser was ruling at the time and asked Imhotep to create a funerary monument for him. The result was the Step-Pyramid at Saqqara.

For the third and fourth dynasties, Egypt was considered a place of prosperity and peace. It was also the time when most of the pyramids were built. This age started to end towards the 5th and 6th dynasties, and the wealth of the King was starting to disappear due to the expensive pyramid building. Power was also starting to falter for the Pharaohs with more nobility and priests taking over the power stating that the Sun God Ra was the true power. At the end of the 6th dynasty King Pepy II died. He was in rule for nearly 94 years.

The period Egyptologists call Ancient Egypt ended when Alexander the Great defeated the Persian Empire. Alexander ruled Egypt until his death then Ptolemy took over control, leaving his descendants in charge. The last Ptolemaic Egyptian ruler was Cleopatra VII - she surrendered to Octavian, known later as Augustus in 31 BC, leaving Egypt under Roman rule for six centuries. When Arabs defeated Roman rulers in the 7th century AD, Islam was introduced to the country and most of the Egyptian way of life disappeared.

Egypt was not the only civilization to be advancing in 5000 BC. Numerous cultures around the world started to settle, to use their own concepts of agriculture and to trade between various cities as trade routes started to open up. China, Egypt,

Europe, and even early civilizations in the Americas existed. But what fascinates us the most about the Ancient Egyptian culture is their advancement in various areas including agriculture, architecture, women's roles and politics. Think about how women are treated in certain cultures even today. Remember how recently American women won the right to vote, and then consider the daily life of Egyptians over 5000 centuries ago that you will learn about in this book.

Keep in mind these other cultures as you explore the daily life, pyramids, architecture, dynasties and Pharaohs of ancient Egypt. Consider what life might be like today if Egyptian ways of life had survived instead of being stamped out by Alexander the Great and the Islamic rule. It is the advancements of ancient Egypt that truly grab Egyptologists attention.

© Copyright 2016 by From Hero To Zero - All rights reserved.

This document is geared towards providing exact and reliable information in regards to the topic and issue covered. The publication is sold with the idea that the publisher is not required to render accounting, officially permitted, or otherwise, qualified services. If advice is necessary, legal or professional, a practiced individual in the profession should be ordered.

- From a Declaration of Principles which was accepted and approved equally by a Committee of the American Bar Association and a Committee of Publishers and Associations.

In no way is it legal to reproduce, duplicate, or transmit any part of this document in either electronic means or in printed format. Recording of this publication is strictly prohibited and any storage of this document is not allowed unless with written permission from the publisher. All rights reserved.

The information provided herein is stated to be truthful and consistent, in that any liability, in terms of inattention or otherwise, by any usage or abuse of any policies, processes, or directions contained within is the solitary and utter responsibility of the recipient reader. Under no circumstances will any legal responsibility or blame be held against the publisher for any reparation, damages, or monetary loss due to the information herein, either directly or indirectly.

Respective authors own all copyrights not held by the publisher.

The information herein is offered for informational purposes solely, and is universal as so. The presentation of the information is without contract or any type of guarantee assurance.

The trademarks that are used are without any consent, and the publication of the trademark is without permission or backing by the trademark owner. All trademarks and brands within this book are for clarifying purposes only and are the owned by the owners themselves, not affiliated with this document.

Chapter 1:
Daily Life in Ancient Egypt

Archaeology gives us a mere glimpse into the past of Ancient Egypt and the Egyptian lifestyle. Many tomb paintings and hieroglyphic texts offer a look into the elitist world, but barely provide any details of regular daily life. Many countries may have been run by Kings and Queens, but it was the peasantry that made up the trade, crafts and food supply any civilization ran on. It was the same for the Egyptians. Pharaohs provided rules and laws, but it was the peasants' daily activities that ensured the wealthy could truly live in comfort. If not for peasants running farms, creating crafts and becoming trades people, the wealthy would have had to spend time doing these 'mundane' chores.

It is difficult to determine the true daily life of regular Egyptians because many scribes wrote about the 'important' people of Egypt rather than the day to day people. However, there are certain things archaeologists have been able to surmise about life as a regular Egyptian.

Marriage

The Egyptians had to marry early in their lives. Living to an age of 40 for most was not possible, particularly in the peasant class. The lack of food, the excess of hard work, and the toll of the desert made it difficult for most to survive. There were a few Pharaohs who lived to be quite old- one in particular ruled for nearly 94 years, according to archaeological evidence. Most women would be married off when they came into maturity or childbearing age.

The Nuclear Family

A nuclear family or elementary family is one that consists of a pair of adults and their children. Many Egyptians had a nuclear family dynamic, where one man and one woman supported the family. This is not to say that the Egyptians were monogamous. Many marriages were polygamous; however there was always a chief wife who was higher in the hierarchy than any of the others and was responsible for the day to day running of the household.

The Husband's Role

The husband was the man responsible for the economic well-being of the family. He was the person who would go out and run the farm, hold a job or work for the wealthy.

The husband was raised to respect his father and to become a husband who would be obeyed by the wives he took. Men could be slaves, servants or craftsmen. Most craftsmen learned their trade from their fathers or from artisans willing to take on an apprentice.

The Wife's Role

Depending on whether the family had more than one wife, the role for the chief wife was always to run the household. Contrary to what one might think, women were treated with respect. They could have opinions, make statements and be treated as equals. More than a few daughters of powerful men held positions, such as Nefertiti and Cleopatra. In fact women could own property, conduct business like men and testify in court. Women would raise the children and prepare the meals, yet still be seen as equals.

It was a necessity in households to have more than one wife, not just a desire by the husband. Wives bore children, and children worked in the house and fields. The role of all the wives and not just the chief wife was to rear the children, and to help ensure they could live long and help their fathers. There would be times when more than one wife gave birth within a few days or months of another.

Children

A husband could have many children. They were a "blessing from the gods," especially in royal and noble families. Pictures left behind show King Akhenaten and Queen Nefertiti loving their six daughters.

Children played very little in Egypt. There are some remnants and pictures that show children playing sports and with handmade toys, but these children were more likely from wealthier families.

The children of peasants would have had to work when they were old enough to understand the job they needed to do. For male children, this was normally farming or apprenticing as a tradesman in their father's business. For female children, it was about learning the household - how to run it, how to make food and how to be a good wife. The cycle would continue, with the daughters finding husbands when they were of marriageable age, and the men working the fields until it was time to find wives and build their own family.

Children in wealthy families would be given an education. This formal education allowed privileged children to become army officers or scribes.

The Working Life

As with many cultures of this time period, there were definite class distinctions. Those who were born to privilege were able to live comfortable lives with slaves or servants to do their work. The peasants had to live using agricultural techniques to grow food such as wheat to survive. A few of the peasants were lucky enough to have grazing lands where they were able to raise meat; however, these peasants often needed to sell the meat they raised to subsist. This meant they ate the wheat and some of the meagre vegetables they could grow in the desert.

Some families were lucky enough to have ox-drawn plows for their plowing, planting and harvesting, but even then the life was a tough one.

Peasants could not hope to raise their class status. Marriage between different social classes was not acceptable in most instances. Additionally, the expense of living life was too great for peasants to be able to save money and raise their social class. Taxes were imposed on all crops because the land was owned by the King, and the peasants were granted the right to use it to make a life.

Scholars find it difficult to determine the true way of life for most peasants, slaves and servants because of contradictory texts and little available information. It has been theorized that slaves were more like servants in most households. Yet it is known that slave labor was used to build the pyramids, so there were people who worked in degrading and humiliating positions.

Food and Beverages

Besides wheat for food, most peasants relied on beer. It was brewed from barley, using processes very similar to the ones we have today. For higher classes, meat and wine were on the table. The other common food amongst all classes was bread. The bread was seasoned with honey, sesame seeds, fruit and herbs.

Dwellings

Clearly the Pharaohs and upper classes had palatial homes. The remnants of these homes in pictures and in ruins are easily seen today. Peasants were not as lucky with their homes. Most homes were adobe (building materials made from the earth and organic materials) to keep the interior of the homes cool in the hot sun. Sun dried mud was used to create the adobe exteriors, which had doors and windows covered with mats as a way to keep out insects and flies. For nobles, the home was divided into three parts: a reception area, private quarters and a hall.

Peasants had what would be considered town homes today, with two or three stories. The first floor of the town home was for business or receiving people. The top floor or two would be private housing based on the amount of family members the peasant had. The roofs of these buildings were flat, enabling Egyptians to sleep outdoors in the hotter months.

At first mud and papyrus were used to construct homes, but soon child labor using children from about 4 years old and up was used to create actual bricks for the adobe dwellings. In most cases, peasants had one room to live and sleep in, with a ramp or ladder to go from the bottom service area to the top floor or the roof.

The lack of plumbing meant sewage was dumped either in the rivers, or in the streets or pits. The downside was that the water Egyptians had to use to live with came from these rivers. The buckets would be used to bring water in for drinking, bathing and cooking, then either be tossed out into the streets, back into the rivers, or into pits constructed for sewage purposes.

There was one thing that made families lucky- if they were pyramid workers. Homes were provided for pyramid workers because these individuals were too busy working on giant structures for the Kings to be able to take care of the building of their own places.

Homes for Richer Families

It is known that richer families actually had stone houses, using materials such as granite, which could be locked from the inside. There have been keys that date to 1550 BC. These wealthier families painted their homes white to help keep the homes cooler during the day. Artists were often hired to paint the inside walls to bring a fresh look to the home. Some of the richest families had 30 rooms with even bathrooms inside, although these rooms lacked running water. Bars were used in richer homes to ensure wild animals and intruders remained outside. Master suites for the husband, along with a toilet area, were made in some of the richest homes. Pipes from gardens led into the bathroom to bring in fresh water, although it was not like the running water of today.

These rich homes held mirrors, pots, pans, shelves, beds, heat, fountains, lighting, cosmetics, perfume pots and various sets of clean clothing. A lot of the homes had gardens and pools containing fish, and flowers that could bloom in Egypt.

Wealthy households held parties, with plenty of food and beverages. Music was also incorporated into these parties. The children of these families had toys carved into shapes like horses, balls and animals. There were also a few board games called Hounds and Jackals, and Senet.

Daily Life and the Nile

Life revolved around the Nile for everyone. It didn't matter if a person was wealthy or not, the Nile was the best source of fish and water and was the easiest way to travel. Along the banks of the Nile were rich areas of fertile soil that were necessary to help people survive.

Each year for three months, the Nile would flood. The waters would fill the crop land with much needed water, allowing the wheat and other crops to grow. It also ensured villages and cities could be built around the Nile.

The Nile provided papyrus reeds. Some families took these reeds to make paper or building materials. When the water receded, they still had the ability to get water into buckets and back to the cities and villages.

Fashion in Daily Life

For men, children and women, clothing was a necessity because of the hot sun. Some children just had enough cloth to cover their important areas, while wealthier families would wear robes made of linen, which also included headdresses. Makeup was also a part of everyday life, no matter the class because it helped protect peoples' skin from the damage sun could do.

Bathing was important as a daily ritual, either in the river or in bath basins at home. Cleansing cream made with lime, oil and perfume was used rather than soap, but they were able to keep clean and hygienic.

Jewelry was just as important to people as the clothing worn. Amulets and rings for religious purposes were worn by most Egyptians; even peasants had simple earrings, amulets and bracelets. Wealthier families had beaded collars, pendants and jewelry of Electrum, silver and gold.

When you consider the daily life of peasants and wealthier Egyptians there are certain cultural lessons to be learned.

- Women were respected, unlike certain cultures of today – a far contrast between the fights for the rights to vote that happened in European and American cultures in more modern day.

- Women may have borne children and run the households, but they also conducted business, were allowed in the courts and were important to the family dynamic.

- Bathing was a must, not something to be feared. Egyptians may not have understood hygiene the way we do now, but they knew using perfume was hardly enough to keep them clean. They bathed every day, unlike later European cultures.

Obviously, there were some deficiencies when it came to sewage and keeping their main water source clean of defecation, and using slave labor for building pyramids. However, it is difficult to argue with some methods Egyptians had in their daily life. They knew what could be grown in their area, how to keep their homes cooler and how to fish for protein. It did not take very long for better homes to be built, or for geometric shapes to be constructed that have lasted millennia for us to see.

Chapter 2:
Pyramids and Monuments of Egypt

The pyramids and monuments of Egypt that exist for tourists to see today were built over three millennia, by several dynastic rulers. Many of these structures have withstood the test of time- the sand, the sun and the sandstorms that may have obliterated entire groups of people did not destroy the structures. Unfortunately, not all structures remain in perfect condition. Pollution from tour buses and decades of exploration have all weakened the pyramids and monuments that exist in Egypt. There are even a few architectural wonders that have been covered and uncovered a few times due to sandstorms.

Step-Pyramid at Saqqara

Archaeologists also refer to this as the Step-Pyramid of Djoser, since he was the Pharaoh in charge of the first pyramid to be built. Its construction was designed specifically to inter Djoser upon his death. Originally the building was a flat roofed mastaba; however, when Imhotep finished the structure, it had increased to six layers and was what we now call a pyramid. It stood 204 feet high. Like the original mastaba tombs of earlier Egyptians, the burial chamber for Djoser is underground. There is a maze of tunnels that were hidden by the structure, but that have now been uncovered by archaeologists.

The Bent Pyramid

The Bent Pyramid or Southern Shining Pyramid was constructed during the 4th dynasty, circa 2600 BC. It stands 344 feet tall, with 617 feet at its base width. Pharaoh Snefru had this pyramid built 40 kilometers south of Cairo in Dahshur, which is known as the royal necropolis of Dashur. It was the second pyramid Snefru requested during his reign.

At first the pyramid begins a 54 degree angle, but this marvel became 43 degrees at the top giving it a bent appearance and thus its modern name. It is long believed by archaeologists that the pyramid was created by a transition from step pyramids to smooth sided pyramids, which lends to the change in angles. The Red Pyramid, which was the third to be constructed by Snefru's rule, is a complete 43-degree angle structure of smooth walls and is why most believe the Bent Pyramid was a transition between the two types of pyramids.

The Bent Pyramid is also considered unique because the outer limestone shell is mostly intact, which is very different from most of the other 90 pyramids and monuments. Scholars believe the limestone was undamaged over time because of the clearances between the outer casing and the expansion joints. The construction allowed for thermal expansion of the outer casing that other pyramids were unable to undergo.

Great Pyramid at Giza

The Great Pyramid at Giza or the Giza Necropolis is in the southwest area of Cairo. It has become the most famous Egyptian temple. It took three generations for the pyramid to be finished. It was started by Khufu, and Khafre and Menkaure added their input during 2500 BC. This pyramid is considered the oldest and the only remnant of the Seven Wonders of the Ancient World to still exist. Archaeologists know more than 2 million stone blocks were used to build the temple over 20 years. The pyramid is 455 feet tall, making it the tallest pyramid in Egypt. This pyramid is also known as The Great Pyramid of Khufu or The Great Pyramid of Cheops. It contains three burial chambers. The first chamber is underground, and the second is above ground and considered the queen's chamber. The third chamber was for the King, which had a red granite sarcophagus in the center of the pyramid, housing his mummified corpse.

Khufu was the son of Snefru.

Great Sphinx at Giza

The Great Sphinx might be the only one mentioned in many books, but it is hardly the only one in Egypt. Its sheer size and location on the Giza Plateau are responsible for its notoriety above the avenue of sphinxes that existed at the Luxor Temple. The Great Sphinx is definitely one of the oldest and largest monuments of Egypt and of the world. Construction began in 2500 BC under the rule of Pharaoh Khafre. The Sphinx has the head of a human, but a lion's body. It is also mentioned in the story of Oedipus Rex. The statue is 241 feet long and 66.34 feet tall.

The Valley of the Kings

The Valley of the Kings is considered the royal necropolis located near Luxor and Thebes. During the New Kingdom, from 1539 to 1075 BC, the Valley of the Kings was used as a royal burial ground for important Pharaohs, Queens, and high priests. There were also several elites, who were wealthy people, buried in the tombs here. It is the burial location for Ramesses II, Seti I, and Tutankhamun. The tombs are the best representation that we have of religious and burial beliefs of ancient Egyptians. In these hallowed halls, mummification was performed preparing the wealthy elitists for the afterlife. For approximately 500 years the tombs were constructed in the Valley of the Kings. The area has 63 tombs and chambers, which all range in size from a simple pit to a tomb with more than 120 chambers. These chambers were decorated with Egyptian mythological symbolism. The downside of the great tombs was the pillaging early discoverers conducted, robbing the tombs of amazing artefacts. King Tut's tomb was the only tomb that did not see the extreme damage by these early looters.

The Temple of Hatshepsut

Hatshepsut, a female ruler of Egypt, was in charge from 1479 until her death in 1458 BC. The Temple of Hatshepsut was erected as a mortuary temple in honor of her. It is located on the west bank of the Nile below the cliffs at Deir el Bahari. This temple is a colonnade structure designed by Senemut. Senemut was a royal architect during Hatshepsut's rule. The temple existed for posthumous worship and to honor Amun. Using the cliffs, the structure was built in three layered terraces. It reaches a total of 97 feet in height. There are two long ramps, which reach the first and second levels. This area around the ramps was once a garden space, long gone due to the changes in nature over the years.

The Luxor Temple

Thebes was established as a city on the east bank of the Nile River. The city was founded in approximately 3200 BC. During this time, it was more of a trading post than a grand location. However, it started to expand during the Middle Kingdom, particularly when the Karnak Temple complex was established. A statue of Nysuerre, a Pharaoh of the 5th dynasty, was constructed in the city and another statue was added during the 12th dynasty to represent Pharaoh Senursret. Thebes was ruled by people said to be descendants of the Prince of Thebes. Other rulers included Mentuhotep II and

Amenemhat I. In Thebes the god Amun was worshiped, with a temple dedicated to this god.

In 1400 BC the Luxor Temple was built in Thebes. This time period is considered to be part of the New Kingdom. The temple was built to worship Amun, Chons, and Mut. All three were very important gods of the time. The temple was placed at the center of the Opet Festival, where the statues of the gods were escorted into the Luxor Temple, along an avenue of sphinxes, which connected an earlier Amun temple and the Luxor Temple.

The Abu Simbel Temples

Located in Nubia and under the Aswan Governorate rule of Egypt sit two temples built circa 1264 BC. Ramesses II requested these great temples be built as a monument to him and his queen Nefertari. He wanted to commemorate his victory during the Battle of Kadesh. The temples sit above the Aswan High Dam today, but they were originally in the path of Lake Nasser. A huge relocation process was undergone to preserve the temples, but also to create the Lake. The temples are built of rock, having been carved from the mountainside. The relocation process occurred in the 1960s, so visitors can still see the great temples on a visit to the area.

Karnak

Karnak is another New Kingdom creation from circa 1570 to 1100 BC. Karnak is a religious site and the largest ancient site of its type in the entire world. Several generations of Egyptian builders worked on the site to create the three main temples of Karnak. There are also smaller temples and outer temples that make up the site, which is 2.5 kilometers north of Luxor. The most famous area of Karnak is the Hypostyle Hall. The hall is 50,000 square feet, with 134 columns in 16 rows.

The Temple of Ramesses III

Medinet Habu is considered the temple of Ramesses III. It was built after Hatshepsut and Tutmosis III built temples in the same area. Ramesses III wanted his mortuary temple to be the largest structure in the area, and made sure it included workshops, storehouses and residences. The temple is dedicated to Amun, like the other two in the area. The temple became an administrative location for Western Thebes, and included a fortified wall and gateway to ensure it was safe from any military action from the Syrians. Ramesses III was a military man, which is probably why he wanted his royal palace and mortuary to be fortified. Today, a lot of the structure has not withstood the test of time- at least in the outbuildings and along all sides of the wall. There was once a harbor entrance that connected a canal with the Nile, but the desert covered this long ago. Medinet Habu was extended for several centuries by the Romans and Greeks. During the 1st through the 9th centuries AD the area was expanded and the temple was used as a Christian church.

Colossi of Memnon

During 1350 BC, the Colossi of Memnon were erected. They are two stone statues, both representing Pharaoh Amenhotep III. These colossi are meant to guard Amenhotep's mortuary temple. They were worshipped before and after his death. The temples and Amenhotep's resting place were largely destroyed by time; however, the statues remain, highly damaged and nearly featureless, but nevertheless still standing.

The Temple of Seti I

The Pharaoh Seti I is honored at the Temple of Seti I. It is a mortuary temple located at Abydos, on the west bank of the River Nile. The construction of this temple was started just before Seti I's death sometime around 1279 BC. Ramesses the Great, Seti's son, took over the construction of the temple. One of the most interesting facts about this temple is the King List. It shows a chronological list of most Pharaohs starting with Menes and up to Ramesses I.

The Temple of Isis

The Temple of Isis most often refers to the temple started by Ptolemy II and finished by the Roman emperors of the 300s BC. The temple was built to honor the goddess Isis, who was the wife of Osiris and the mother of Horus. The three gods/goddesses dominated Egyptian religion, which may be why Ptolemy II felt it necessary to erect a temple in Isis' honor. The legend says Osiris was murdered by his brother Seth, but Isis collected all dismembered body parts of Osiris and used her magic to bring him back to life. It was then that they conceived Horus. The temple represents the giver of life and is also associated with funeral rites, since she brought Osiris back to life. The temple is near the Aswan Dam, located on an island to save it from the 1960s Lake Nasser project.

The Temple of Kom Ombo

Kom Ombo was built under the direction of Ptolemy VI in the second century BC. There are two temples with symmetrical creation, so the main axis looks duplicated. There are two entrances, two colonnades, two courts and two hypostyle halls. There are also two sanctuaries. The temple has views of the Nile, since it sits on a high dune.

Temple of Edfu

The Temple of Edfu is a place to worship Horus. It is considered the second largest temple, smaller only than Karnak. It is also one of the temples most preserved today. Construction of this temple was also started by Ptolemy III, but was not completed until 57 BC by Ptolemy XII, who was the father of Cleopatra. Many elements of the New Kingdom temples are found within the Temple of Edfu, as well as some Greek elements like the Mammisi or house of birth.

Mastaba Tombs

Prior to the pyramids discussed in this section, the Egyptians had Mastaba Tombs. These tombs were often underground chambers for courtiers and Pharaohs. Mastabas were flat surface structures, with openings on at least two walls. The top brick, with the flat roof, was only meant to cover the opening underground where one would follow stairs to reach the actual burial chambers. Typically, these structures were rectangular in shape with sloping sides.

Chapter 3: Religion, Gods, and Beliefs

Egyptians believed strongly in religion which influenced their traditions. There was a firm belief that natural and supernatural forces existed and that it was these forces that determined the course of life. The cycle of the Nile River flooding for 3 months out of the year, the harshness of the desert and the sun's daily cycle were all attributed to gods and goddesses.

Religion was not something that stayed steadfast through the 5000 year history of ancient Egypt. When lower and upper Egypt united under one ruler, there was a merger of many cultural traditions. Ancient Egyptians were not the only culture to exist, which meant new contact with different people changed their ideas and values.

Osiris was at one time a local deity who ruled the Nile River, but over time he became a countrywide god. Gods such as Re or Ra, the sun god, Khepri of the morning, Horakhty of midday and Atum of the afternoon became central to the ruling power.

Historically, the tradition of rulers was based on divine kingship, where those who ruled were thought to be chosen as the Pharaoh by the gods. Due to the beliefs in Pharaohs being kin to the gods, they held vast power. Priests were also powerful. It was thought that if both the priests and Pharaohs did their jobs well then the country was doing well; however, if things turned bad for the country, then it was the priests and Pharaohs who were at fault.

Depending on the sources one reads regarding religion, there were as many as 2000 gods and goddesses that oversaw the running of Egypt. The culture was polytheistic because they believed in numerous gods, rather than a monotheistic religion where only one god was worshipped.

During the history of Ancient Egypt there was a period while Akhenaten ruled that he tried to instil the monotheistic approach to religion. It did not last because of the deep traditions already in place. Many of the 2000 gods and goddesses worshipped were local gods, and only a handful of them were nationally recognized gods. The people of Egypt looked to the gods for help in most aspects of their daily lives, whether it was for a safe journey into the next life or for help when a woman was bearing a child.

Certain gods and goddesses were more important to the life of the Egyptians and had temples built around them. These are the gods and goddesses discussed in brief:

Amun – he was the creator god from whom all other gods and goddesses came from. This national god rose to the height of popularity when Thebes became the capital city instead of Memphis. At a certain point in Egyptian history, Amun was combined with Ra the sun god to become Amun-Ra. Amun-Ra was the power behind all existence. He was the god the Pharaohs answered to and the one that provided secrets, wind and fertility.

Ra- he was the sun god and the father of all other gods, who was often depicted in ancient art to have the body of a human but the head of a falcon. Many of the temples had Ra either in statue or picture forms.

Horus- he was another sun god and king of all gods. At one point the Pharaoh's title was "The Living Horus" to emphasize that the Pharaohs had the right to rule Egypt like Horus ruled the various gods. Like Ra, Horus was usually depicted as a falcon. He was also considered one of five Osirian gods. Osiris and Isis (Horus' parents) and Set and Nephthys were the other four. The most well-known symbol of Horus was the Eye of Horus, which was a symbol of power.

Isis- Isis was the mother goddess and fertility goddess. Already the legend of Osiris being brought back to life was discussed in relation to her. However, she had many roles and was considered the "goddess with 10,000 names."

Osiris- he was the god of resurrection and of the dead. Osiris was a ruler of Tuat. People worshipped him to help their loved ones depart well. Until Set, his brother, killed him he was also considered the king of gods.

Set or Seth- he was a god of darkness and evil. He was not only an adversary of Osiris, but also of Horus. Set was often called upon in times of war for his strength, and in deserts and storms.

Hathor- she was a cosmic goddess and the goddess of cows. She helped nourish life with her milk, thus she was often called "House of Horus." The legend states Hathor was a consort of Horus. She had a triad between Horus and their son Ihi.

Ma'at- she was a goddess of physical and moral law. Many scholars believe she was important to Ancient Egypt because she was the one who judged the dead. Worshipping her would mean a fair judgement because in life a person would be moral and ethical.

Sobek- he was another god of strength, one who was always seen as a crocodile god or a crocodile with human attributes. Sobek was the strength of the Pharaohs.

Anubis- Anubis is another god often depicted in various media and fanciful stories of modernity; however during the Ancient Egyptians lifetime Anubis was considered the god of dying and death. He was a god of the underworld, a guardian of tombs and of all those entombed within.

There were many more gods and goddesses, but it is these top names that had the most influence over the everyday lives of Egyptians, including the rulers.

Creation Myths

As in most cultures, you should expect Ancient Egypt to have a creation myth or three. In Ancient Egypt, these myths are called Heliopolitan, Memphite and Hermopolitan. Each is named after the city where the creation myth associated with the name was first developed. There is one thing that is at the center of each story—the Island of Creation, a primordial mound of earth.

The creation stories all date back to the Old Kingdom, rather than earlier before the unification of Egypt.

Heliopolitan- this myth believes in Atum Ra or Atum Re as the central god. Atum Ra willed himself to exist. From this god came Shu, who was known as the god of air. Tefnut also arose from Atum Ra to be the god of moisture. These two gods created Geb the earth god and Nut the sky god. From Geb and Nut were formed the elements that could produce Osiris, Seth, Isis, and Nephthys. The Heliopolitan Myth is the most accepted creation myth of Egyptian cultures.

Memphite- this is the second myth that arose when Memphis was created as the capital. Ptah was the creator god of all. Ptah was the one who started the original creation cycle. It was necessary for Ptah to create a daughter, who then created Re-Atum. Ptah, according to the Memphite Myth, created the world, cities, gods, food, drink and all essential items needed for life. However, the Memphite Myth did not gain notoriety among most Egyptians.

Hermopolitan- Hermopolis was the city in which this myth arose. It was said the god of wisdom, Thoth, was the first. However there are also several accounts of this myth. The one that stands out the most was that a group of eight gods that created the world from the primordial ocean. Another account says that there was a cosmic egg that brought life. Thoth was also said to come from a lotus flower, which rose from the 'Sea of Knives.'

While the three myths as outlined above are the most accepted, there were other creation stories too. During the New Kingdom period, Amen Re was said to be the creator of man and gods. The Karnak temple was built in his honor. Yet Elephantine, a ram headed god of Khnum was said to have created man on a potter's wheel.

If one takes a hard look at the beliefs mixed in with the various creation stories, it is evident that one story began it all, and each city worked to adapt the story to fit the lives in that city. It is also fairly clear that many of the cultures in Europe and Africa started out believing in multiple gods, which was very different from other cultures who believed in one supreme being.

The Role of Priests

Priests were very important to religion, both in how it spread and the myths that were believed in. The temples were erected for the gods to live in. Since the temples were extremely sacred, only priests were allowed to enter them. Priests could approach statues of gods and goddesses to pay their respects and hold special rites to honor these various deities. Regular people could come to the gate or to the Pharaoh's court and pray to the gods. The Pharaoh would act as a go-between for the people to speak with the gods, or for the gods to communicate to the people.

The Priests existed to care for the goddesses and gods. They did not or should not have a hand in caring for the people of Egypt. Unlike other religions, priests of Egypt did not educate people on religious practices or ensure Egyptians followed moral lives.

According to scholars, priests would rise in the morning, break the seal to the area, light torches to walk the gods and say prayers. They would wash the statues, provide fresh clothing and jewels to be worn and leave offerings. Hymns would be sung throughout the day. At the end of the day, the priest would follow the footprints that brought him in, seal the area and leave the gods and goddesses in peace.

Several records of early Egyptian life indicate the people believed that their lives would be in turmoil if the priests did not fulfil their duties to the gods. If famine, plague or drought occurred, then it was because of the priests. To ensure the priests would not neglect their duties, they were paid handsomely. Most priests worked on a rotational system because they were not full time helpers. Instead, there were usually four priests that would take care of one sacred area -

these groups would serve for a month before going back to their occupation as a government official for three months.

The Pharaohs had the power to choose new priests. It meant relatives would usually fill these positions and rise in power and influence over the people. More than often priest positions were hereditary, meaning that they would be inherited by family members unless the Pharaoh saw a need for power to be transferred. For certain priests a committee of priests hired replacements; however this did not happen often.

Priests were held to certain requirements when working in the sacred areas. For example, they could wear only linens or clothing made from plants. Any clothing made from animals was not permitted. Priests had to shave their heads and bodies on a daily basis. Cold water baths were a must, several times each day, and sexual abstinence while working at the temple was a necessity.

It was from their beliefs in gods and goddesses as well as their overall religious beliefs that brought about the concept of mummification and the preservation of the body for the afterlife.

The Cult of Osiris

Abydos became a cult center where people would come to worship Osiris. A temple was built in dedication to him and each year a procession of people would come, carrying an image of Osiris from the temple to a tomb. It was believed that the tomb held Osiris; however it is now known that the tomb held either Djer or one of his relatives. It is known that the cult started to form in lower Egypt near the delta. Historians believe that Osiris might have been a real king, but this is unproven. It is known that many believed in the god Osiris, who ruled the underworld after he was brought back to life. The cult spread throughout Egypt, with little opposition to stop it. Religion and the gods were considered very important to daily life, so why not honor a god who could protect the departed? The Osiris cult appealed more to the lower classes and the peasants.

There was a thought that if Osiris could resurrect, then perhaps regeneration into something better could be possible. Each Egyptian wanted eternal life, but without the means of mummification it was not possible for lower classes to believe they would be protected.

Naturally, when a cult started spreading in honor of Osiris, it started to make sense to the peasants to do all they could for their afterlife. It was also thought that the materials used for mummification, which you will learn about later, were made from the tears Osiris shed as he died.

Since Osiris was honored with a cult, it also made sense for Isis to be a star with her own cult following. Isis was the one responsible for piecing Osiris back together so it was she who could grant life again, while Osiris could protect and offer eternal life to all those who lived in Egypt.

Chapter 4:
Burial Customs

Since the dawn of humankind, it has been necessary to take care of the remains of loved ones. Archaeologists can show how many civilizations cared for their family members, as far back as the Neanderthals. Unarguably, the Egyptians have one of the most advanced and complicated processes for the burial of their dead.

Burials did not start out complicated. Like many early cultures of the world the Egyptians would lay their dead in a grave, often in a foetal position, and cover the body. As civilization evolved, so did their process of burials. Kings and wealthier courtiers wanted more than just a ground burial. Around the time of the unification of Egypt, Mastaba tombs were starting to appear. The downside to Mastaba tombs was a lack of preservation. Without sand, often filled with salt for preservation, the bodies were not being saved. The family would come to honor their ancestors but find rotted bodies inside the moist, cool interiors of the Mastaba tombs.

It was a long process for the Egyptians to learn better burial customs for their dead. The process used in the New Kingdom for mummification was quite different than the original process.

Old Kingdom Mummification

Mummification started out as a process for drying and preparing the body for better preservation, so family members could honor their dead properly. During the Old Kingdom periods bodies were most likely dried in the sun with Natron salt. To prevent the bodies from separating, linen was used after the drying process. Some of the earliest mummies, which have been uncovered by archaeologists, show a plaster was used for some wrappings instead of linen. The plaster would be molded to the person's body to preserve what they looked like.

About the time of the first pyramid, the Step Pyramid, in the 4th dynasty, mummification took on the process of embalming. Embalmers would remove the internal organs. There are texts and mummies which show the trial and error embalmers went through to provide the perfect mummification process.

New Kingdom Mummification

By the time the New Kingdom dynasties rolled around, mummification was at its peak in terms of use and practice. However Pharaohs, royal families and the wealthiest of people were the only ones who could afford the preservation process. It is known that commoners and peasants were still buried in sand cemeteries, which means they went through the natural mummification process created by the dry climate.

It was not the process of mummification that took a great deal of the wealthy and royal kitties. It had more to do with the Mastabas, which became pyramids, which then housed great artistry, jewels, and other wealthy items. The wealthy felt they needed grand houses that would have everything useful to them in the afterlife.

The sarcophagi that were created for the wealthy were often made from precious metals and plaster. The grand platform where the sarcophagi were placed would also make for an expensive building process. Everything that went into the burial custom to preserve the dead for the afterlife is what made it unobtainable for the peasant class.

Afterlife

The entire reason for the preservation of Egyptian bodies was their views on the afterlife. Egyptians firmly believed that the body was linked to the spiritual existence of the person. The body had to be preserved so the spirit would be able to get drinks and food in the afterlife. If a body was destroyed or damaged in some way, such as a horrible death, priests would perform magic spells on statues so that the spirit of the deceased person had a place to go for their afterlife needs to be met.

It did not matter whether one was wealthy or not, families would honor their dead by bringing food, drink and other belongings to the spirit to ensure they had a peaceful afterlife.

Three processes of mummification were created. The first was the most common and will be discussed in more detail. The second mummification process used cedar oil, which was injected into the body through the rectum before the body was dried with Natron salt. The third method of mummification used an injection of an unknown liquid before the body was dried with the salt compound. Egyptologists have been unable to identify what the liquid was used in the third method.

The Book of the Dead

The Book of the Dead was a true book that existed. It was a book of scripts left for the dead. It contained magical spells that would guide spirits through the afterlife since the journey could be a most difficult one to navigate.

Like many stories of the dead reaching a point of rest, the Egyptians believed that there was a river the spirit would have to cross. It was a wide river. The journey across the river would end at a gate, where the spirits would pass through. The gate was guarded by monsters.

Upon entering from the gate, the deceased person would be in the Hall of Two Truths where they would be judged by the appropriate god and goddess. The person would have to stand trial in court, where they were accused of 42 different crimes. The person would need to answer to these charges by using his heart on one scale and a feather on the other.

If the heart was lighter than the feather the person would move passed the hall of judgement and join the gods. If the heart was heavier than the feather, the person was filled with deceit. A monster would devour the heart leaving the person without personality or memory, and thus without a chance for eternal life.

The goal of all Egyptians was to gain eternal life, which also meant that their body had to be preserved to ensure they could live in this comfortable afterlife.

The Process of Mummification

There were three Egyptians usually involved in the process of mummification. There was a scribe, a cutter and an embalmer. The scribes would oversee the cutter. The cutter would make incisions in order to remove the organs. Since the cutter's job was unclean - dealing with the dead bodies and cutting them open – most of them were not allowed to have much of a position in society.

The embalmer was different. This person was usually a priest who would remove the internal organs and prepare the body for the full mummification process.

Typically, the work would be done in a workshop close to the site of the tomb. Mummification took at least two months before the deceased could be properly buried in their tomb.

The process would begin with the body being stripped of its clothing and placed on a board. A special tool was used to extract the brain through the nose, leaving the skull empty until resin could fill the space. Often a combination of resin and linen was used to ensure the skull was completely full.

The cutter would open the chest, often with the Y incision still used today. All the main organs would be removed except the heart. All organs removed would be placed in Canopic jars with their own drying agent. Typically, there were four jars to represent the four sons of Horus.

The organs were not always placed in the jars and set aside. In some cases the organs would be wrapped in four packages and placed back in the abdominal area. Some priests wrapped the organs and put them on the mummy's legs. The different procedures for the organs usually depended on the time period one referenced in Egyptian history. The heart was never removed from the body.

Whether the organs were placed back inside the body or not, the next part of the mummification process was to wash the empty body cavity and pack it with Natron salt. The body would be left to dry for around 40 days. After the body had dried and if the organs were placed back inside, the body was then sewn up. The cut would be sealed with wax or sometimes metal.

In certain processes, the bodies were filled with sawdust, linens, salt or ash in order to keep the bodies firm after they had been dried. The eye sockets were most often filled with linen, but in certain periods of the Egyptian timeline fake eyeballs were used.

The body would be cleaned again after it was stitched back together and was then wrapped in linen. It was always a thick layer of fabric that would be wrapped around the body. As soon as the outside layer of linen was wrapped, the body was transported to the tomb.

The body could not be put to rest before a burial mask was placed over it. The burial mask most individuals call to mind when hearing about this process is the mask found on King Tut. It was the most elaborate mask. After the mask was put in place the body was put into the sarcophagus or coffin, which would protect the body further from damage.

The more money or privilege a person had, the more elaborate the decorations were on the sarcophagi. Some archaeologists believe the sarcophagi may have been put into several more casket layers before the body was placed in its final resting place.

Chapter 5:
Animals, Beliefs, and Mummification

Today animals fit into two categories: food or companions. Dogs and cats have been domesticated as companions, as have other animals. Fish, birds and cows are used for food. In other cultures, like Ancient Egypt, some animals were used for survival purposes and others were associated with gods and goddesses. Some of these animals were used for sacrificial purposes and others were deified based on the beliefs of Egyptians that certain animals were representations of deities.

The following animals were important to the Egyptians:

Cattle

Cattle were the main source of meat; however, the cow was also associated with fertility. The bull or male cow was associated with power, fertility, masculinity and regeneration. Cows and bulls were often slaughtered as sacrificial offerings to the goddesses and gods of Egypt.

Pigs

Pigs were considered chaos, light and sacrifice. Most pigs were used for oil and fat in cooking. Pigs were not made a part of sacrifices like the cattle were.

Goose

Geese were used for their eggs. The goose was also attributed to gods and goddesses like Isis, Geb and Amon.

Sheep

Animals that fit in the sheep and goat families were in some ways considered very important. The ram was always recognized by ancient Egyptians as an animal representing Khnum and Banebdjedet. Sheep and goats were thought to be associated with strength, fertility and birth.

Donkeys

Donkeys were used in processions, to pull chariots and for hunting. Donkeys and horses were both revered and expensive, so horses were considered a status symbol.

Wild Animals

The above animals were domesticated for the Egyptians to use as food or work animals. There were also wild animals that were considered to have religious associations. For example, antelopes were considered very important to Sokar. The heads were put on the prows of ceremonial boats at temple sanctuaries. The baboon was supposed to be an animal of strength, eloquence, responsibility and fairness. The baboon was closely associated with Thoth, as well as with Khonsu and Hapy. Thoth was responsible for the yearly calendar based on the lunar cycle, thus he was often shown to have a baboon head in pictographs.

Crocodiles were wild animals of justice. Perhaps the legend started when someone who was unjust fell into the jaws of a crocodile. What is known for certain is that three gods were associated with power, justice and respect: Sobek, Taweret, and Amnut. It was said that Amnut, the demon god with a Crocodile head, would eat sinners' hearts as a means of punishment for any sin they conducted during their lives.

Crocodiles were actually fed and cared for in sacred lakes because they were so revered.

All snakes were important to the Egyptians- most particularly, the cobra. The cobra represented Wadjet, as well as justice, protection, fertility and royalty. Snakes were often seen in pictographs to represent resurrection. It is known that snakes are difficult to kill. Unless the head is removed, snakes can still move. According to one tale Methen, a giant snake, guarded the boat of Re when he would go to the underworld.

Frogs were another animal related to fertility, childbirth and resurrection. Heget, Ogdoad gods, Nun, Amen, Heh, and Kek were all represented by frogs. Perhaps it is the sheer abundance of frogs that made them important to the lives of the Egyptians or the fact that frogs can change their sex to meet the needs of their population.

The lion is an animal that was once plentiful in all of Africa, and was associated with the gods. Lions represented leadership, strength, ferocity, royalty, war, beauty and healing. Aker, the earth god, was often shown as a double sphinx who would guard the sun when it came and went from the underworld.

The scarab beetle was a special insect revered for its dung and the ability of its young to rise from that dung to create new life.

The monkey (not the baboon mentioned earlier) was also considered an important animal. The gods were said to transform into monkeys to walk around the earth. The monkey was seen as a symbol for renewal and rebirth.

Birds

The Egyptians didn't leave any species out of their religious beliefs if one considers the domesticated animals, wild animals and birds they held in high esteem. Falcons and hawks were often associated with Montu, Horus and Socar. These birds were thought to offer protection, royalty and strength. Many of the gods were usually drawn with falcon heads, as were some of the Pharaohs. In some cases, the Pharaohs had falcons with outstretched wings designed into the throne or over the head of the throne to show they were chosen by the gods to rule.

The Ibis was definitely an important bird. The Ibis was usually mummified when it died and buried in the catacombs and tombs. The Ibis was associated with Thoth, Djehuty and Tehuty. It was also considered a representation of the soul and of knowledge. All the gods associated with this bird were known as writers, magicians or teachers.

Vultures and ostrich were also personified. Vultures were meant to show eternity due to the outstretched talons that would offer protection to the Pharaohs, drawn on the temple ceilings. Ostriches were associated with Ma'at, who had an ostrich feather in her hat. Several Egyptian women followed this same style.

Cats

Cats deserve their own section apart from the domesticated animal lists because Egyptians seemed to revere the cat the most among all animal species. Cats were the only companions in a sea of various animals. They were also a symbol that represented Bastet and Ra. Scholars believe that the Egyptians thought cats held divine powers. Cats were often seen as protective and tender, thus pregnant women would have cat amulets or Bastet amulets with kittens to ensure a safe pregnancy and delivery.

Cats, along with the Ibis, were two of the animals interred in tombs; mummified like their owners. Cats were provided a high level of respect in life and death, which meant they were protected. Killing a cat would mean the death penalty. So much was the belief in cats that Egyptian men would rescue cats if a fire broke out. If a cat tried to run into the flames there were men specifically in attendance to ensure they did not succeed.

Cats were so revered that each year thousands of Egyptians would travel to Bubastis to owner Bastet. The cats would also be wrapped in linen and taken to Bubastit, where the mummification process would take place before the cats were buried in a special, sacred cemetery.

Dogs

Dogs were not as revered as cats; however many families of wealth had dogs they used for hunting. Dogs were not seen as mystical or as important as cats. It was actually the loyalty of the dog to its owner that made it seem extremely low, nothing more than a servant to some. It was an insult if someone called another person a dog. Yet the dog was associated with Anubis, who was considered the god of mummification and embalming. Since the dog was associated with Anubis, it was also mummified and placed with other sacred animals.

Mummification of Animals

Any animal that underwent mummification would go through the same process as a human, although it would not take as long since the animal was smaller. The organs would be removed by cutting open the animal. Then the animal would be dried for several days, until it was finally sewn up, stuffed with linen and preserved in wrapped linen. In many cases the animal would be buried in a sacred cemetery like the location at Bubastit. However, if an owner died, an animal would often be killed so it could follow this person into the afterlife. When this occurred the animal was usually buried with the person in the same sarcophagus or nearby in the same chamber.

While it was illegal to kill a cat for no purpose, it was seen as just to help the animal follow its owner into the afterlife. Depending on the Egyptian the animal might have lived past their life, but then be mummified and placed in the same chamber so it could then follow the owner later on.

It was the religious beliefs that the Egyptians had in animals, gods and goddesses that made it possible for animals to be preserved along with important Egyptians of the time.

Chapter 6:
Festivals

Ancient Egyptians had secret temple rituals and annual festivals. There is a list of 50 different festivals and rituals conducted in the name of religion that occurred during a calendar year. For the Egyptians, a calendar was 360 days long. The other five days were spent worshipping the five sacred gods: Osiris, Horus, Isis, Seth, and Nephthys.

To understand more about the religious beliefs and the gods worshipped by the Ancient Egyptians, it is helpful to examine the four most important festivals. These festivals are Wepet Renpet, The Sed Festival, Opet Festival, and the Festival of the Beautiful Meeting.

Wepet Renpet

The translation of these words means 'opening of the year.' It is considered Egyptian New Year, a day celebrated in connection with the Nile River's floods each year. The New Year was usually celebrated in July, when the river would first start to rise. The flooding of the river meant fertility would reach the farmlands. The appropriate flooding ensured the New Year would be prosperous. Communities would come together, celebrate with feasts and pray for a good year for their crops.

The Festival of the Beautiful Meeting

This festival is still held today in honor of Horus and his marriage to Hathor. The statue of Horus at Edfu was always taken to the place of Hathor's statue. Hathor's statue was taken from the Dendera River Bank, approximately 100 miles away from the Horus statue. This part of the celebration does not go on today; however the feasts with free food and drink for all the people are still performed. The festival was truly one to honor marriage- the marriage of two gods and the marriage of Egyptians. The idea that people could meet and marry for the happiness of their life is still a worthy celebration.

The Sed Festival

Known as the Heb Sed Feast of the Tail, the Sed Festival was always celebrated when a new pharaoh reached their 30th year of rule. The festival was then held every 3 years until the pharaoh's rule ended, usually due to death. Sed Festivals were held in several temples throughout Egypt, with various rituals, offerings, and the adjed -rising the spine of a dead cow to show the strength of the pharaoh. A feast was always offered during this festival to ensure the pharaoh would have continued strength throughout his rule.

The Opet Festival

The Opet Festival was held as a Theban Triad celebration. The festival was always held on the 19th day of the second month of the first season in the Egyptian calendar (Lee, Demand Media). It was the second month called Akhet. When the festival was held statues of the triad of gods were brought from the temple by boat. The statues would leave Amun and go the Luxor Temple. During the journey down the Nile, the boat would stop at chapels in the community to receive the offerings people in the area were bringing to the procession.

For three weeks the statues would remain at the Luxor Temple, before being taken back to their respective locations in Karnak. The statues would remain in their home location until the next Opet Festival was held.

The Egyptians had more than these four festivals. These were just the four most important and well-known. Another festival held by the Ancient Egyptians was the Festival of Khoiak.

The Festival of Khoiak

This was considered a festival of sustenance, originating from the myths surrounding Osiris. It all comes back to the legend where Osiris was killed by his brother Seth, but brought to life by Isis. The death and revival required an observed festival, always held in the fourth month of the year right after the flood season was over. Once the Nile was back to its usual level, the Egyptians would shape the earth in Osiris' profile. Seeds were planted in Osiris beds, and these would be the crops guaranteed to flourish in the year just as Osiris was able to flourish again after death.

A look at the festival calendar as it would have been during the Ancient Egyptian time period shows many festivals were held in the first couple of months. For example:

- In month one of the new year, offerings were made to Hapy and Amun on the 15th day to ensure a good flood occurred. Two days later was the Wag Festival that would last until day 19, and then the 20th was the Tekh or drunkenness festival, with the month finishing on the 22nd with the Great Procession of Osiris festival.

- The second month of the New Year had the most festivals, starting on the 15th and ending on the 28th. These included Ipet, which was an 11-day festival for Amun held in Luxor. There was a river procession for this festival in which offerings were made to Ipet. A local festival held on Day 18 was called the Elephantine Festival of Khnum. It was a festival to honor Khnum and Anuqet. Many of these festivals started during the Middle Kingdom period.

- In the third month on Day 9 the Egyptians held a festival for Amun. There was also another Elephantine festival for Anuqet on the 30th day.

The calendar was made up of four-month periods, which were given names and festivals associated with the time of year. For example, the first four months of the New Year were called the Season of Flood. The next four-month period was the Season of Sowing. It should be mentioned that each month in the new season was called Month 1 2 3 and 4. In the Season of Sowing, month four was a festival for Bast- a day of chewing onions for Bast, who was said to make an appearance on day 5 while in her boat. There were harvest and granary offerings made during these months.

The next season was known as the Season of Summer. Several festivals like the adoration of Anubis and Festival of the Valley were celebrated during the four months of this season. The Festival of the Valley always celebrated the new moon in the 2nd month. The great festival was held at the Theban Necropolis, with Amun of Karnak as one of the main gods celebrated. It was a festival of flowers, for families to provide a feast for their dead and to decorate tomb chapels.

The aforementioned five days, which were celebrated not as part of the 360 days but as five separate days, were considered birthdays. Day 1 was always for the birth of Osiris, the second was for Horus, the third for Seth, and the fourth for Isis. The fifth day was a birthday celebration of Nephthys.

Chapter 7:
Pharaohs and Dynasties

Chunks of time in Ancient Egyptian history usually fall into certain categories: Early Dynastic, Old Kingdom, First Intermediate, Middle Kingdom, Second Intermediate, New Kingdom, Third Intermediate and Late Period. However, within these categories are 31 dynasties, referred to as pre-Ptolemaic dynasties. There were also some dynasties that were ruled at the same time but in different cities. The concept of dynasties did not come into play until a Ptolemaic Egyptian ruler and priest decided in the 3rd century BC to name the periods dynasties, within the periods already named.

Some of the dynasties are difficult to truly discuss because they are more of a continuation of an earlier dynasty, such as the ninth and tenth dynasties that do not seem all that different. The dynasties were just given a certain period of time to last and thus broken down into that time frame, whether it made sense or not. For some it is easier to consider the pharaohs of the time and try to determine the dynasties they ruled in.

Pre-dynastic Period

In the pre-dynastic period there was lower and upper Egypt. Since there was no unity during this time, there were many rulers. These names are known only because they were discovered by Egyptologists on a Palermo Stone. The names of rulers in Lower Egypt include Seka, Khayu, Tiu, Thesh, Neheb, Wazner and Mekh. These leaders ruled the northern Nile and Nile Delta.

Upper Egypt belonged to the Naqada III period or dynasty 00. The rulers of this time period were Elephant, Bull and Scorpion. Remember all of these rulers existed prior to 3150 BC.

Dynasty 0

Dynasty 0 was considered the dynasty before the First Dynasty and the dynasty of the unification of Egypt. Rulers of this time were Iry-Hor, Crocodile, Ka and Scorpion II. Scorpion II is generally thought to be Narmer. No one can say for sure who Narmer is. There is a debate as to whether he was the one who truly unified Egypt or if it was King Menes. Narmer was known as "the unifier of Egypt" and there are two necropolis seals that show he was the original king of the First Dynasty.

The other debate is that Narmer was actually King Menes and thus was the true unifier of Egypt. No one will know for sure. It is too difficult to determine the past, when various records are missing or have been destroyed. All we can go on is what has resurfaced during archaeological digs. The trouble with dates and pharaohs is that Narmer may have been Scorpion II who lived during 3150 BC, or King Menes who unified Egypt in 3100 BC. There is a large 50-year gap, where one or both men could have died and there may never have been a Narmer. There is a small likelihood that Narmer was a name given to those who tried to unify Egypt rather than the name of the actual person.

The First Dynasty may have been unified, but there were still other pharaohs ruling their own areas. These men were Hor-aha, Djer, Den, Anedjib, Semerkhet, Qa-a, Sneferka and Horus Bird. Qa'a was an important ruler because he lived a very long life. Qa'a ruled for 34 years. His tomb is also the last one with subsidiary tombs.

Rather than list every ruler Egypt had, the following will highlight some of the more important timeframes within dynasties. Hotepsekhemwy or Boethos, depending on the written record, ruled for 15 years. His rule was not a good one in the end. An earthquake killed hundreds of people, which may have been the beginning of some of the superstitions mentioned earlier. A pharaoh that allowed an earthquake would have been considered out of favor with the gods.

Nynetjer was a ruler for 43 to 45 years in the same dynasty as Hotepsekhemwy. It is said that Nynetjer's successors allowed women to rule as if they were pharaohs. Perhaps this is when Egypt realized that women could be seen as equals and not just as child bearers.

Seth-Peribsen was the starter of the sun-cult. He was a pharaoh who did not like other people to have all the power. In fact he started to remove power from officials, palatines, and monarchs. A few scholars believe he was a ruler during a time when Egypt was no longer unified but was in turmoil. There is not enough evidence to say whether this is actually the case or not.

As there were rulers who may have been blamed for natural occurrences like earthquakes, there were also pharaohs who were seen as wonderful because they could end droughts. There is a legend that claims Neferkasokar was able to save Egypt when it was in a deep drought.

Before the Old Kingdom and Third Dynasty began, Khasekhem was the ruler. It is said that he reunified Egypt, perhaps after the trouble that split the kingdom when Seth-Peribsen ruled.

Third Dynasty

The Third Dynasty was extremely important to the Egyptian way of life. Djoser was the first ruler, who may have ruled for 19 or 28 years. You should recognize his name from earlier discussions as the first pharaoh to require pyramids to be built.

He would not live to see the step pyramid finished- Sekhemkhet would start ruling before that happened. Egyptologists found an interesting artefact in his step pyramid. As they dug down to uncover the unfinished step pyramid built for Sekhemkhet, they found a mummified 2-year-old infant.

The history surrounding Huni is just as jumbled as many of the rulers in the Third Dynasty. Huni was thought to have built the Meidum Pyramid; however after digs relating to the New Kingdom it was discovered that King Snofru was responsible for that pyramid. Huni was also credited with an unfinished step pyramid and cult pyramids throughout Egypt. These facts are still in conjecture among scholars.

Sneferu or Snofru came after Huni. He was considered a pious and generous ruler. It is known that he commissioned three pyramids that are still standing today: Meidum, Bent and Red.

Khufu was also a ruler of the Fourth Dynasty. He was responsible for the Great Pyramid of Giza as well as written works on papyrus scrolls. Legend says Khufu spoke with a magician Dedi, in which a prophecy was made. The Greeks long believed the texts left by Khufu were simply trying to please and praise the gods.

The next several dynasties had many rulers, but they were not as important as those who came into the New Kingdom. They are also not remembered as much in the texts and history books as those who came later.

In the 18th Dynasty there was a ruler called Akhenaten. This man was married to Nefertiti. It is not his marriage that holds the most fascination though. Akhenaten tried to change Egypt. He believed in monotheistic Atenism and tried to change religion from the belief in multiple gods. Akhenaten worshiped Aten, a sun disc.

The next name or ruler in this dynasty was Ankhkheperure Smenkhkare. It is not certain if this person was Nefertiti who was given the right to rule alongside her husband or Akenhaten's son Tut. Tutankhamun has his own mysterious background.

We do know that King Tutankhamun did rule from 1333 to 1324 BC. It is also said that he reinstated Polytheistic religion, changing his name from Nebkheperure to Tut. History shows that King Tutankhamun ruled the throne from approximately 8 or 9 years of age and died when he was 18 or 19. Given his early rule, he was nicknamed "The Boy King."

The 19th Dynasty

The next dynasty is another that seems to bring about plenty of stories and mentions in the history books. It is the time of Ramesses and Seti.

This dynasty started in 1292 BC. For those who study other history such as the Trojans and Greeks, you may find some interesting parallels- particularly with the mention of the Hittite Empire.

The first king was Menpehtire Ramesses I, usually called Ramesses. He was not of royal birth but he did succeed Horemheb, since Horemheb did not have an heir. Ramesses showed that he was capable of ruling Egypt and some legends have it that he was 'chosen by the gods' to rule rather than any offspring or relatives of other royalty.

Ramesses I had a son called Seti I. During Akhenaten's rule a lot of territory was lost to opposing forces. Seti I was able to get that territory back during his 11-year reign.

Ramesses II the Great, son of Seti I, was also a great leader. His rule lasted from 1279 to 1213. During this time he expanded Egypt's territory, creating a stalemate with the Hittite Empire during the Battle of Kadesh and was able to get the Egyptian Hittite peace treaty signed.

During these various dynasties not all was well. There were some rulers who tried to usurp the throne from others, as well as some rulers that may have been assassinated like Usermaatre-meryamun Ramesses III.

It is also difficult to determine who was who because a lot of the texts used Ramesses or Seti, with III, V, VI after the name, but not the first name. There are several of Ramesses offspring that certainly didn't live to be 100 hundred years old, which helps in some respects in figuring out who they belong to.

When the Egyptian dynasties came to an end after 31 long periods, the Ptolemaic Dynasty began. This is marked most famously by Julius Caesar, Mark Antony and Cleopatra VII. Cleopatra VII was always known simply as Cleopatra. She could see a change in the world with Rome growing larger and larger, so she tried to create a political union during her rule. Unfortunately, Julius Caesar was assassinated and Marc

Antony was defeated, which ensured her plans never came to fruition. The eldest son of Cleopatra, Caesarion, ruled with Cleopatra until her "suicide." Many texts confirm that Octavian had Caesarion killed. Octavian would become the Roman Emperor and ruler over Egypt—Augustus.

The Legend of King Tut

You may be fascinated with Egyptian lore and history because of the very famous curse of the pharaoh. It is often referred to as King Tut's Curse. King Tut's tomb was found in the Valley of the Kings. It was said that anyone who would violate the final resting place of the boy king would face a terrible curse.

The legend became so widely known because of uncertain deaths that occurred. Several people who found King Tut's tomb died not long after it was opened. It was said in the legend that anyone who opened the tomb would die under mysterious circumstances.

The legend gained notoriety when George Edward Stanhope Herbert died. He was a British Earl as well as an amateur Egyptologist. He financed the search that led to the discovery of King Tut's tomb. Herbert died one year after the tomb was opened. Many would spread the rumor saying it was King Tut getting back at the man; however before Herbert arrived in Cairo he was already in a detrimental health situation. After exhaustive research into the death of this man, it was discovered he died from a mosquito carried illness. This death and others were perpetuated in fictional accounts like that of Sir Arthur Conan Doyle's works.

When trying to assess the validity of the curse, one investigator found that most of the people associated with opening King Tut's tomb during Herbert's explorations died more than 23 years later. Howard Carter, who discovered and opened the tomb, and then removed King Tut's sarcophagus from the chamber so the dead king could meet the public lived sixteen years after his discovery, finally dying in 1939. He died of cancer at age 64.

It is said that the curse story was actually perpetuated by Howard Carter. It was an amazing find, something that had not occurred before. In order to keep away all the people who might disturb the site he perpetuated the myth already in existence.

The Curse Myth

Not only was King Tut's tomb not supposed to be disturbed, but all other royal tombs were supposed to be left alone. Perhaps it was a civilization that came after the Egyptians who had already robbed the tombs and wanted to make sure no one else could take anything of importance. Perhaps it was the Egyptians who warned of dire curses because they knew someone might try to take the gold and other worthy items from the tombs.

Imagine a time when land is being fought over because someone has the better land. The Nile certainly provided a decent way of life and plenty of gold and other riches were known to be amongst the belongings of the wealthy.

In an age when magic and curses were believed, it would be easy to say "if you disturb this 'human god's' afterlife you too shall die". It may also be another case of happenstance.

What would one think if a man found robbing a tomb was killed for no reason they could find? It would definitely perpetuate a myth that any royal tomb disturbed would lead to a mysterious death.

Chapter 8:
Separating Truth from Fiction

At the beginning, it was mentioned that sometimes our fascination with Egypt is a direct result of what we are exposed to, whether it is in a museum or a movie. Museums do their best to provide us with artefacts- whether they are replicas or true artefacts they help us understand a culture or civilization. You know the information you learn in a book or museum is based in fact, but what about the world of movies? Are some of the things we have seen in movies like Cleopatra, The Mummy and The Mummy Returns actually based in fact or are they complete fiction?

The Mummy

You have learned that Imhotep was actually a priest who lived in the first dynasty and was responsible for helping erect the Step Pyramid. Of course, one can surmise that his love for the pharaoh's wife and the plot to murder was not actually true, nor was the possibility of his being resurrected due to a curse. But what about some of the 'lessons' that were shown in the movie about mummification and the city of Hamunaptra - did these things have basis in truth?

One of the first non-factual elements of the movie was the five canopic jars shown in the film. Four were used for the organs of the body and the heart was never removed. The brain was removed, but not with a red-hot poker as stated in the movie. However as the actress was holding the real device, it was never heated up.

Based on the religious information learned in the above chapters, you should also be aware that the greatest punishment for any criminal of any class would be to not allow mummification, since mummification was designed to grant the person eternal life.

Hamunaptra was not a real city, but one of fiction. Pharaohs were usually buried in Saqqara or Abydos in the earlier Egyptian dynasties.

Scarab beetles were considered important to the ancient Egyptians, but they never ate human flesh. They ate their own dung.

When it comes to the two books discussed in the movie, you know that the Book of the Dead did exist as a bunch of scripts left to guide people into the afterlife. It was not made of gold or any other precious metal, but was more likely in the form of a scroll. There was also a Book of Thoth. The Book of Thoth was considered a book that contained all the education of the Egyptians, including remedies for healing and magic, and was said to be written on papyrus scrolls. Setna, the son of Rameses the Great, was a great scholar who embarked on finding the scroll. The scroll was said to be buried in a tomb in Memphis with the creator, Nefrekeptah. The legend surrounding this book stated that the book was worthless and the wisdom written no longer important to the time when Setna lived. It was deemed a book that would bring him trouble. Of course, this is just another legend and may have been some of the foundation for the golden book mentioned in The Mummy.

The Mummy Returns

When it comes to movies, the writers are more than happy to borrow information from a long period of time and make it into one story. We do know that the Scorpion King existed, but it was well before Imhotep was alive and a priest. The Scorpion King tried to unify Egypt, but failed and several years later King Menes made it a reality.

One also has to look at a few of the characters like Nefertiti and Anck-Su-Namun. Ankhesenamun, as it can be seen spelled, was an Egyptian queen who lived somewhere between 1348 and 1322. She was a queen of the 18th dynasty. She was also one of six daughters born to Akhenaten and Nefertiti. You might already understand where this is going.

Firstly the plot takes a man- the Scorpion King from before the dynasties of Egypt began- and then the plot takes the daughter and pits her against the mother. In the film Ankhesenamun was supposedly the wife of the current pharaoh, and Nefertiti was his daughter. So the historical account does not make sense, since Imhotep would have been long dead before either woman was born and the Scorpion King would also have been dead before Imhotep was a priest.

Knowing these facts should not change the entertainment value in the films; however, it is always interesting to conduct a comparison to see just how far the plot has strayed from history.

Cleopatra

The movie released in 1963 was supposed to be a representation of the great queen Cleopatra, who came towards the end of the Egyptian dynasties. Cleopatra - like many movies - lacks in historical content. A couple of things that have been noticed about the movie that are not historically accurate - the forum depicted in the film is smaller than the true forum in reality. Cleopatra is also seen walking through the Arc of Constantine, but the arc was not built until well after her death. The Roman Legionaries outfits were from a century later.

Like the Mummy movies, there were several fictional elements that were 'based on' facts from the time Cleopatra lived. In the movie they showed Cleopatra as pregnant and defying the Romans, yet Cleopatra did succumb to the Romans – she even carried a child for Caesar and then left behind three children, who belonged to Marc Antony.

A lot of the trouble with the fiction in the movies is that it becomes romantic fiction rather than giving the true picture of daily life as an Egyptian in these various times. Still, for those who enjoy a little romance, it can also help bring about one's fascination for the real culture that existed several thousand years ago.

At least you can now say with that the characters in the films were based on real people, if only slightly taken out of context for when they lived, died and what they truly accomplished in life.

Conclusion

Thank you again for purchasing this book!

I hope this book was able to help you with your needs and to satisfy your reading pleasures. Egypt has always been a fascinating country to study, not only for its geometrical shaped pyramids that were far more advanced than any other country, but also for its people.

The Egyptians held women in esteem, as equals, capable of running businesses, testifying in court and bearing children. Somewhere along the way, many civilizations seemed to have forgotten about this way of life. Many European countries treated women as the weaker sex, yet they were considered mothers and in charge of the household. A question to leave you with is why. Why did the Egyptian way of life, where women were treated well disappear? Why did the world become a place where women were considered shunned, weaker, or incapable of education?

Perhaps the answer lies in the fact that the Egyptian way of life was not as persistent as the Ptolemaic rule, which was then overtaken by Islamic rule in the end.

What you do know and understand now is the daily life many Egyptians led. You have learnt about the religious beliefs that created festivals, burial customs and the belief in polytheistic gods versus one god having all the power to create the world.

Egypt will always be shrouded in a little mystery. How can it not be, when we are still looking for answers? Egyptologists are still trying to find all the artefacts pillaged by earlier explorers and grave robbers. They are also still working to uncover some of the structures and tombs that are completely covered by the sand. As with any culture we may never have all the answers, but we can thank the scribes and artists who were decorating tombs and temple walls for the vast knowledge that we do have.

Hopefully this book was able to answer a few questions you have about Egyptian history and you can now look forward to learning more about the individual gods and goddesses that were only highlighted in these pages. Perhaps the next time you visit a museum with an Egyptian display, you will find more answers or be able to put some of the information you learned to use by comparing what you learned with actual artefacts.

Finally, if you enjoyed this book, please take the time to share your thoughts and post a review on Amazon. It would be greatly appreciated!

Thank you and good luck!

Preview Of 'Egyptian Gods The Gods and Goddesses of Ancient Egypt'

Introduction

Ancient Egypt has held humanity in its thrall for over 5000 years. The image of the Great Pyramids of the Valley of the Kings rising ghostlike from the white sands of the Sahara Desert is synonymous with the mysteries of the Ancient World.

Ancient Egypt was remarkably advanced, especially considering its origins date back 30 centuries before the Common Era. From clocks to the 12-month calendar to agriculture and fashion, we continue to experience the echoes of Ancient Egypt in the world we live in today.

The Ancient Egyptians had a religion worthy of the complexity and advanced nature of their society. Ancient Egyptian religion formed a link the animism of prehistoric Hunter - Gatherer tribes with the complex pantheons that would follow, like the ancient Greeks and Romans. Ancient Egypt's religion also bridged the gap between paganism - believing the Gods and spirits could be supplicated and appealed to - and the non-interventionist spirituality of the Abrahamic religions of Judaism, Christianity, and Islam. Ancient Egyptian religion would even help give rise to monotheism, after a brief flirtation with Atenism during the 18th Pharaonic Dynasty, which only lasted 20 years before being erased from history.

Religion was incredibly important to the Ancient Egyptians, making up much of the fabric of their lives. The Ancient Egyptians believed that the Gods' favor could be swayed through acts of sacrifice, prayer, and magic. The Ancient

Egyptians allocated intense amounts of resources to the construction of temples and religious centers, in keeping with the importance they placed on immortality and the afterlife.

Although the Ancient Egyptian religion is cloaked in the symbolism of myth - with chimerical Gods featuring animal heads on human bodies - it actually illustrates the beginnings of scientific thought, as the Ancient Egyptians sought to make sense of the forces of the natural world that shape their life.

On the surface, a pregnant woman with the head of a hippopotamus and the antiseptic world of the scientific laboratory couldn't have less in common, seemingly coming from different galaxies. And yet, looking at the Gods of the Ancient Egyptians is like watching the birth of modernity.

To fully know ourselves, we must understand where we come from. The animal-headed Gods of the Ancient Egyptians are a fascinating place to begin. So let us part the mists of time and return to Luxor, to Memphis and Thebes. Say a prayer to the scarab, light some sandalwood, and let us begin.

The Gods of the Ancient Egyptians

Ammit

Hieroglyphics:

Role: Demon

Title: Devourer of the Dead

Ammit (alt. spellings Ammet, Ammut, Amam, Amemet, Ahemait) is a demon who dwells in the Hall Of Ma'at, with the body of a lion or other big cat, the hindquarters of a hippopotamus, and the head of a crocodile. Ammit's name literally translates to "Devourer", which earned her many titles over the millennia, like "Devourer Of The Dead", "Soul Eater", "Demoness Of Death", "Devourer Of Millions", or "Devourer Who Dwell In Amenta," a valley west of the River Nile where many cemeteries were located.

There are no rites associated with Ammit, as she was not worshipped. Ammit was the personification of chaos and disorder; a representation of all that the Ancient Egyptians feared and hated. She resides in the Hall Of Truth, dwelling beneath the Scales of Ma'at, where Osiris weighs the heart of the deceased against a feather from Ma'at's headdress by Anubis. If a heart is found to be heavier than the feather, the heart is given to Ammit to eat, dooming the deceased to the Ancient Egyptians' worst fear - the "second death", or eternal restlessness. (See Also: Anubis, Ma'at, Osiris)

In some versions, the condemned are swallowed whole by Ammit, doomed to forever digest in Ammit's stomach. Some believe this could be an early incarnation of the Christian ideal of the Lake Of Fire.

Ammit's appearance is a reflection of her role as devourer, being a composite of the most vicious animals in Egypt. Ammit is also associated with Tawaret, the hippopotamus goddess responsible for warding off evil, and Sekhmet, goddess of the sun and fire, due to her lioness aspect.

Although Ammit was feared and regarded as a demon, her role illustrates the complexities of Ancient Egyptian religion. She punishes the wicked and, as such, can be seen as an agent of good. She is a representation to follow the laws of Ma'at, or divine justice and harmony.

Amun - Ra

Hieroglyphics:

Role: God

Title: King of the Gods, King of the Wind, Hidden One, The Great Cackler, The Hidden Light

Spouse: Amaunet

Capital: Thebes

Amun - Ra is one of the most important deities in the Ancient Egyptian pantheon. In his original incarnation as Amun, he was included in the earliest Egyptian cosmogony - the Ogdoad - eight divinities worshipped in Hermopolis in the Old Kingdom between 2686 to 2134 BCE. Amun - Ra is perceived as one of the gods responsible for creating the world from the chaos of Nun, or primeval waters.

Amun - Ra is visualized most frequently as a bearded man, sitting on a throne, with the Ankh of life in one hand and a scepter in the other. He wears a cup on his head, surrounded by two red ostrich feathers. He can also transform into a goose, earning him the title "The Great Cackler", as well as a human with the head of a frog or cobra. He is sometimes depicted as a human with a ram's head, symbolizing his role as God Of Fertility. During the Ptolemaic Dynasty, he is depicted as a man with four arms, the wings of a hawk, and the paws of a lion.

Amun - Ra's role in the Ancient Egyptian cosmology grew and evolved over time. The original 8 Gods and Goddesses of the Ogdoad were elemental figures with very little personification. There was hardly any difference between the Gods and Goddesses.

Over thousands of years, Amun's mythology grew and expanded. A patron saint of Thebes, Amun gained further importance when he absorbed the local God Montu, a God of war, in the 11th Dynasty. His position grew more exalted during the Middle Kingdom (2000 - 1700 BCE), when the Theban chief Ahmose I evicted the Hyskos, a group of Asiatic people that conquered the Nile delta for a time. To commemorate their victory, the royal family commissioned a number of temples to be built to the divinity, most notable the Great Temple At Karnak and the Luxor Temple.

Amun came close to being Egypt's sole divinity during Egypt's New Kingdom (1550 - 1070 BCE) when he fused with the sun god Ra to become Amun - Ra, or "the hidden light". Amun - Ra's influence was so great it even spread out of the country, into Nubia, and Amun - Ra was considered an equal of Zeus by the Greeks. Pharaohs were said to be "beloved of Amun - Ra", as were their queens. Queen Nefertiti was granted the title "God's Wife of Amun". The prevalence of Amun - Ra's cult would help to increase the role of women in Ancient Egyptian society.

A celebration of Amun - Ra, the Opet Festival, is one of the most significant events of Ancient Egypt. During the festival, a bull-headed statue of the deity travels from Luxor to Karnak, to commemorate his marriage to Mut, with whom he sired Khonsu, the God Of The Moon. The bull-head is a representation of Amun - Ra as God of fertility.

Amun - Ra is also important in the Gnostic tradition, represented by Abraxas.

There are more stories of Amun - Ra and Osiris than any other male deities, both of whom are referred to as King Of The Gods.

Amazon US

Link: http://www.amazon.com/dp/B017W44098

Amazon UK

Link: http://www.amazon.co.uk/dp/B017W44098

Made in the USA
Middletown, DE
11 January 2018